HRJC

THE STORY BEHIND

TIME

Elizabeth Raum

Heinemann Library
Chicago, Illinois

To order:
☎ Phone 888-454-2279
🖳 Visit www.heinemannraintree.com
  to browse our catalog and order online.

Edited by Louise Galpine, Megan Cotugno,
  and Laura Knowles
Designed by Philippa Jenkins and Artistix
Original illustrations © Capstone Global Library, LLC 2009
Illustrated by Geof Ward
Picture research by Mica Brancic and Elaine Willis
Originated by Modern Age Repro House Ltd.
Printed in China by CTPS

13 12 11 10 09
10 9 8 7 6 5 4 3 2 1

Library of Congress Cataloging-in-Publication Data
Raum, Elizabeth.
  The story behind time / Elizabeth Raum.
    p. cm. -- (True stories)
  Includes bibliographical references and index.
  ISBN 978-1-4329-2343-3 (hc)
  1. Time. 2. Time--History. I. Title.
  QB209.R39 2008
  529--dc22
                          2008037393

Acknowledgments
The author and publishers are grateful to the following for
permission to reproduce copyright material: Corbis pp. **4**
(© Louie Psihoyos), **14** (© JJamArt), **15** (© Bettmann),
21 (© John Heseltine), **22** (Brand X/© Colin Anderson),
23 (© Reuters) **25–26** (© Bettmann); © DK Images p.
19; Getty Images pp. **6** (Collection Mix: Subjects/Code
Red), **7** (Taxi/Bill Losh), **8** (Riser/© B2M Productions), **9**
(© Science Faction/Yoav Levy), **10** (© Patricio Robles Gil/
Sierra Madre/Minden Pictures), **16** (Stone/© Hugh Sitton),
18 (© Three Lions), **27** (AFP/© JOHN MACDOUGALL);
© Mary Evans Picture Library 2008 p. **17**; © Photolibrary.
com p. **13** (Imagestate RM/Pictor); Shutterstock pp. **iii**
(© stocksnapp), **12** (© Tamara Kulikova); The Bridgeman
Art Library p. **24** (© Bildarchiv Steffens).

Cover photograph of of inner works of a watch reproduced
with permission of Getty Images (Stockbyte/© John Foxx).

Contents

Some words are shown in bold, **like this**.
You can find out what they mean by
looking in the glossary.

The Beginning of Time

▲ This geologist learns about Earth's past by measuring dinosaur footprints high in the Andes Mountains of Argentina.

Time is a way to measure the past, the present, and the future. We can tell day from night, winter from summer, and young from old. Most people know their exact age. But how do we know the age of Earth itself?

How old is Earth?

Scientists have divided Earth's history into time periods called **eras** (see chart opposite). These scientists, called **geologists**, made their decisions by studying rocks and the fossils (remains) of plants and animals. The earliest era is called the Precambrian Era. This was a long time ago. During almost all of this era there were no plants or animals living on Earth.

13,700 BYA
The "dawn of time" occurs.

4,500 BYA-544 MYA
The Precambrian Era begins and ends.

14,000 BILLION YEARS AGO (BYA)

4,000 BYA

Geologists believe that the earliest animal and plant life began on Earth during the Paleozoic Era. Fish of various kinds lived in the water. Plants, including large trees, grew on land. The Mesozoic Era was the time of dinosaurs. Crocodiles, birds, snakes, and early **mammals** lived then, too. It was not until the Cenozoic Era that many of the plants and animals common today began to appear on Earth. Scientists now believe that humans have lived on Earth for about 1.8 million years.

Ideas Change

In the 1600s, people believed that Earth was created in 4004 BCE. That would have made it about 5,600 years old at the time. During the 1700s, a French scientist believed that Earth was at least 75,000 years old. Today, geologists study rocks and fossils to learn Earth's age. Scientists now know that Earth is billions of years old.

▼ This chart shows the history of **geologic time**. (BYA means "billion years ago." MYA means "million years ago.")

Era	Characteristics
Dawn of time (13,700 BYA)	The universe is formed.
Precambrian (4,500 BYA–544 MYA)	Earth is formed. There are poison gases in the atmosphere (the air surrounding Earth) There is a cold climate (weather conditions) with glaciers (large masses of ice). The first, very simple plants and animals form.
Paleozoic (544–245 MYA)	There are jawless fish, hard-shelled creatures called trilobites, the first land plants, early spiders, and fish with bones. There are the first signs of sharks, **reptiles**, and insects (some with wings). There are cone-bearing trees.
Mesozoic (245–65 MYA)	There are dinosaurs, crocodiles, marine reptiles, turtles, mammals, birds, crabs, frogs, and salamanders.
Cenozoic (65 MYA–today)	Dinosaurs disappear. There is an increase in types of flowering plants, small mammals, trees, first grasses, camels, cats, dogs, horses, and rodents. Homo sapiens (modern humans) appear.

544-245 MYA
The Paleozoic Era begins and ends.

245-65 MYA
The Mesozoic Era begins and ends.

65 MYA
The Cenozoic Era begins. It continues through today.

1.8 MYA
Human beings appear.

500 MYA   400 MYA   300 MYA   200 MYA   100 MYA   0 MYA

Biological Clocks

▲ Some jobs require people to work at night. It is difficult to adjust to a new schedule.

From the beginning of their time on Earth, humans have had special ways of telling time. These built-in clocks are called **biological clocks**. They tell humans when to sleep and when to eat. Scientists have discovered a tiny clump of **cells** in the human brain that tells the body what to do when. These cells help control breathing, temperature, and other things. They tell the heart to beat in a regular rhythm or pattern. The pulse at a person's neck or wrist is a body clock.

Temperature Matters

Human body temperature is lowest around 5 o'clock in the morning. As people wake up, their temperature rises. The stomach prepares to digest the food that will soon be eaten at breakfast. Body temperature continues to rise until just after lunch. Then it drops slightly. It rises again until about 7 or 8 o'clock at night.

Scientists continue to study the human brain to learn more about the biological clock. They hope to discover ways to improve health and safety.

A human day

Humans spend about one-third of their lives sleeping. Scientists at Harvard University in Cambridge, Massachusetts, studied people's body temperature. People's body temperature rose and fell over time in a regular pattern. The pattern repeated itself every 24 hours and 11 minutes. Scientists called this pattern a day. This happened no matter when people went to bed or woke up.

▼ Even if people eat well and exercise, they will still grow old.

▲ Children who do not get enough sleep at night may fall asleep in school or be too tired to learn.

Losing Sleep

Over half of all adults say they have trouble sleeping at least a few nights a week. Elementary school students may have problems, too. A recent study showed that students in grades 1 to 5 got about 9.5 hours of sleep. Some children need a full 10 hours of sleep each night. Some need even more. Lack of sleep makes learning more difficult.

What about you?

Doctors suggest that drinking soda with caffeine may cause some children to sleep less. (Caffeine is a chemical that keeps people awake.) Many sleep experts also believe that children who watch too much television may have trouble sleeping. About half of all school-aged children have a television in their bedroom. Is that a good idea? Do you think that drinking soda or watching television causes sleep problems for you?

Age	Sleep needs
Newborn babies	16-18 hours a day
Preschool children	10-12 hours a day
School children and teens	9-10 hours a day
Adults	7-8 hours a day

How much sleep do people need? ✔

Getting enough sleep is important for good health. Sleep needs change as a person gets older. Also, some people need less sleep than others.

▼ Scientists who study sleep are performing tests on this young woman. Sensors attached to her head measure her heart rate, eye movements, and brain waves.

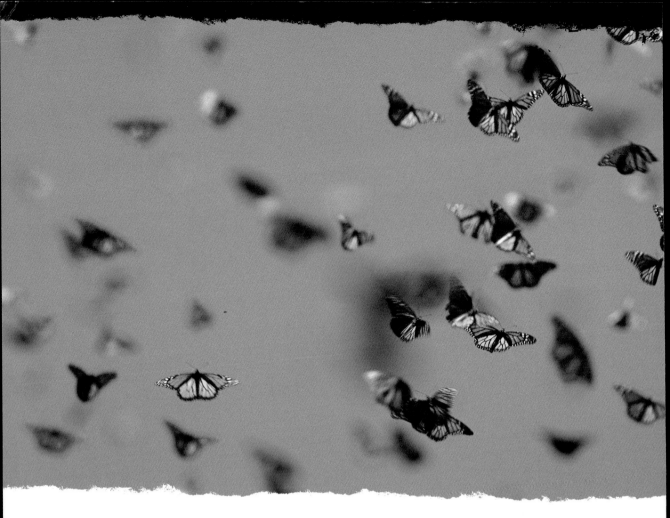

▲ Millions of monarch butterflies travel from the northern United States and Canada to Mexico every fall to escape cold weather. In the spring, they return north.

Animal clocks

Animals have biological clocks, too. These internal clocks tell animals what to do. They make roosters crow each morning and squirrels gather nuts to store for the winter. Bears know when to hibernate (sleep) for the winter. Scientists have studied jellyfish, worms, starfish, and spiders. They have also studied rats, kangaroos, cats, and many other creatures to learn about biological clocks.

Solar eclipse

A solar eclipse occurs when the moon passes between Earth and the sun. Darkness falls over Earth, making daytime seem like night. Insects fall asleep and birds stop singing. Animals go to their burrows or dens. The eclipse fools their biological clocks into thinking it is night.

Flowers we can count on

Plants have biological clocks, too. Each fall, many trees lose their leaves. In the spring, the weather warms up. Then new leaves grow. In 1751 Swedish scientist Carl Linnaeus pointed out different kinds of flowers. Some change their opening and closing times depending on the weather. Others change their opening and closing times as the length of the day changes. Some, like the morning glory, open and close at the exact same time each day. Other plants, like some bamboo plants, hardly ever flower. When they do, they all flower at the same time across the whole world.

▼ The morning glory opens at exactly 5:00 a.m. and closes by evening.

A Short History of Time

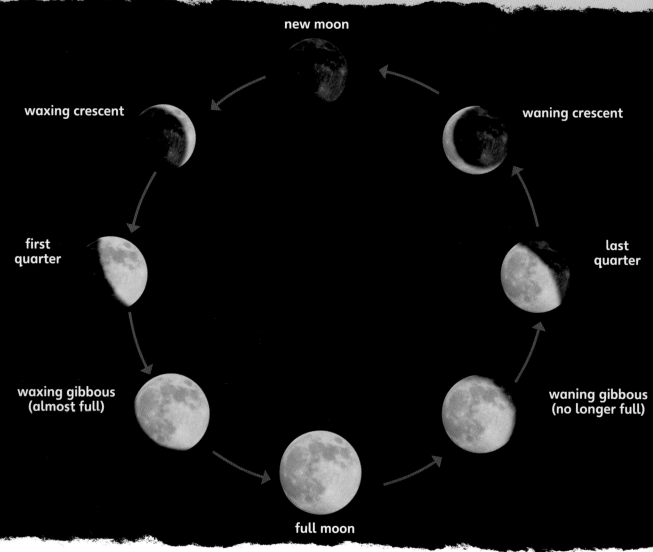

new moon

waxing crescent

waning crescent

first quarter

last quarter

waxing gibbous (almost full)

waning gibbous (no longer full)

full moon

▲ Earth's moon goes through eight different phases as increasing (waxing) or decreasing (waning) amounts of its surface are lit up by the Sun.

It is easy to tell whether it is night or day by looking out the window. It is much more difficult to know the length of a week or a year. Ancient people noticed that it took the moon about 30 days to go through its **phases** (see diagram). They made **lunar calendars** based on the phases of the moon. Farmers used these calendars to decide when to plant crops.

4241 BCE
The Egyptians use a lunar calender.

Egypt's calendar

The lunar calendar had an average of 354 days. But it takes Earth 365.2422 days to revolve completely around the sun. That is an 11-day difference. Egyptian farmers were planting about 11 days earlier each year. Over time, they were planting when it was still cold. Their crops suffered because the seasons are actually based on the cycles of the sun rather than the moon.

In 2772 BCE (about 4,800 years ago), the Egyptians switched to a calendar based on the sun. It was called a **solar calendar**. Each new year began with the rising of the star Sirius. This happened every year just before the spring floods. Farmers depended on solar calendars to plant crops.

▼ **Some people believe that these huge standing stones at Stonehenge in England may have been a kind of calendar.**

3000 BCE	**2772 BCE**
Builders begin creating Stonehenge.	The Egyptians switch to a solar calender.

3000 BCE

2000 BCE

13

▲ Many ancient people developed calendars. This is what the Mayan calendar looked like. It had 18 months of 20 days, with 5 extra days for holidays. The ancient Mayans lived in present-day Mexico and Central America.

Julian calendar

Beginning in 753 BCE (about 2,800 years ago), the Romans used a solar calendar. They added extra days or months to make the calendar work. In 46 BCE Rome's ruler, Julius Caesar, wanted a better calendar. The new calendar had 12 months. Each month had either 30 or 31 days. This all equaled 365 days in a year. Every fourth year, February would have an extra day. This is called a leap year.

753 BCE
The first Roman calendar is made, with a seven day week.

46 BCE
The Julian calendar is created.

500 BCE   0   500 CE

Gregorian calendar

Tiny differences may not matter at first. But after 1,500 years, the difference between the sun's year (365.2422 days) and the Roman year (365.25) added up to 10 days. The calendar dates did not match the seasons.

In 1582 CE, Pope Gregory XIII developed the Gregorian calendar. It dropped 10 days off the old solar calendar. This is the calendar used today. Its calendar year is only 0.0003 days longer than the sun's year. People who use the Gregorian calendar will never have to drop days again. Instead, they will skip three leap years every 400 years to keep the calendar on track.

Some places adopted the new calendar right away. Others, like the American colonies and Great Britain, waited until 1752. They had to drop 11 days from their calendars. Japan and China waited even longer to make the change.

▼ Companies often give away free calendars to advertise products. This calendar is from the year 1894.

1582
The Gregorian calendar is created.

1752
The Gregorian calendar is adopted in the American colonies and Great Britain.

1873
The Gregorian calendar is adopted in Japan.

1949
The Gregorian calendar is adopted in China.

1000   1500   2000

Obelisks and sundials

Today, clocks and watches divide time into hours, minutes, and seconds. However, the first clocks measured hours only.

Ancient people noticed that the Sun crossed the sky each day. It made shadows of different lengths on the ground. About 3500 BCE (5,500 years ago), the Egyptians built tall four-sided stone towers to tell time. These towers were called **obelisks**. Later, smaller versions called sundials were used throughout the ancient world. Sundials and obelisks cast a shadow on the ground. People used the length of the shadow to tell the hour. Sundials and obelisks do not work at night.

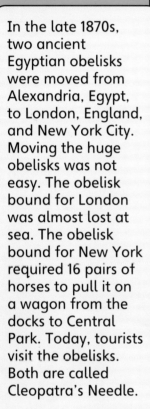

Cleopatra's Needle ✔

In the late 1870s, two ancient Egyptian obelisks were moved from Alexandria, Egypt, to London, England, and New York City. Moving the huge obelisks was not easy. The obelisk bound for London was almost lost at sea. The obelisk bound for New York required 16 pairs of horses to pull it on a wagon from the docks to Central Park. Today, tourists visit the obelisks. Both are called Cleopatra's Needle.

▶ This Egyptian obelisk used the Sun to tell time.

3500 BCE
Egyptian obelisks help people tell time.

Water clocks

Water clocks told time both day and night. They measured time by how long it took a stream of water to fill a jug. Some water clocks used a series of jars or buckets. Others tipped over, ringing a bell when full.

Water clocks had problems, too. In cold areas, the water froze. In warm areas, it evaporated (turned from a liquid into a gas). People needed a better way to tell time.

◀ This Chinese water clock was used during the 1300s.

200-1300 CE
The Chinese use water clocks.

0

1000 CE

2000

17

Tick tock

In about 1285, the first ticking clocks came into use in Italy. These clocks used **gears** to move the hour hand forward. The gears ticked as they moved. These early clocks did not keep exact time. In 1509 German locksmith Peter Henlein used a spring to power clocks. This made smaller clocks possible.

Pendulum clocks

In about 1582, the Italian **astronomer** Galileo developed the idea of the **pendulum**, or swinging weight. He timed the swinging arms of a chandelier (light) hanging from the ceiling. He realized that the time it took to swing from one side to another was always the same. A Dutch astronomer named Christiaan Huygens used this idea to build a pendulum clock in 1656.

▶ **Christiaan Huygens built the first pendulum clock in about 1656.**

1285
The first ticking clocks are built.

1509
German locksmith Peter Henlein uses springs to power clocks.

1000   1500

In 1761 British inventor John Harrison made a pendulum clock that could keep almost exact time, even on a rolling ship at sea. It also gave sea captains a way to know where they were.

Over time, clocks became smaller and more accurate. By the 1800s, many clocks ran on batteries. Later, they used **alternating current electricity**.

Watch clubs ✓

In the late 1800s, working people in the United States and England formed watch clubs. Watches were expensive, so each member of the club paid a small amount each week. The club bought one watch with the money. Members drew names to see who got the watch. The club continued until all members owned watches.

▼ This diagram shows how the swinging pendulum (green and orange arms) turns the gears that move the clock hands forward.

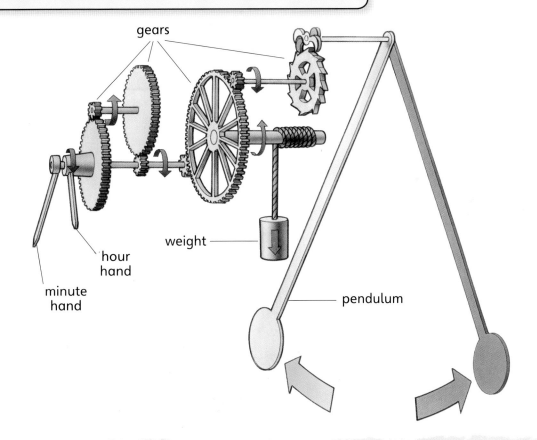

gears

hour hand

minute hand

weight

pendulum

1656
Dutch astronomer Christiaan Huygens invents the pendulum clock.

1761
British inventor John Harrison invents a ship's clock.

19

2000

World Time

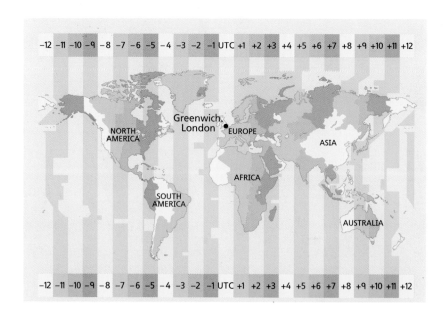

Jet lag ✓

People who fly overseas may suffer from jet lag, also called time zone change syndrome. They may feel sad, tired, and have an upset stomach. They may have trouble sleeping. It takes about a day for the body to adjust to each time zone change.

During the early 1800s, towns and cities kept their own time. This caused problems when railroads began to grow. Passengers had to reset their watches often because each town clock was slightly different.

Standard time

Great Britain was the first country to adopt standard time. By 1852 most British clocks were set to the time in Greenwich. (Greenwich is now a part of the city of London, England.)

The United States and Canada were too big to use a single time for every town. In 1882 Canadian inventor Sandford Fleming, who worked for the Canadian railroad, had an idea. He suggested that the world be divided into 24 equal **time zones.** Each zone would be one hour different from those on either side.

▶ **This map of the world is divided into the 24 equal time zones. The numbers at the top and bottom of the map show how many hours ahead or behind a zone is from the time in Greenwich, England.**

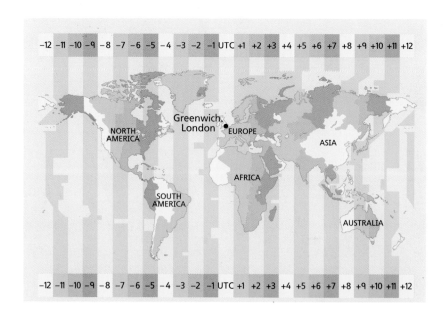

| −12 | −11 | −10 | −9 | −8 | −7 | −6 | −5 | −4 | −3 | −2 | −1 | UTC | +1 | +2 | +3 | +4 | +5 | +6 | +7 | +8 | +9 | +10 | +11 | +12 |

Greenwich, London
NORTH AMERICA
EUROPE
ASIA
AFRICA
SOUTH AMERICA
AUSTRALIA

| −12 | −11 | −10 | −9 | −8 | −7 | −6 | −5 | −4 | −3 | −2 | −1 | UTC | +1 | +2 | +3 | +4 | +5 | +6 | +7 | +8 | +9 | +10 | +11 | +12 |

1852
Great Britain adopts standard time.

1800

1850

In 1884 a conference was held in Washington, D.C. People from all over the world attended. They agreed to Fleming's plan. They chose Greenwich, England, as the place where the official (or standard) time begins each day. Today, this worldwide time system is called Coordinated Universal Time (UTC).

International Date Line

The International Date Line is an imaginary line halfway around the world from Greenwich, in England. This is where each new day begins. The date west of the International Date Line is one day later than the date to the east.

▼ This clock in Greenwich, England, shows Coordinated Universal Time.

1882	1884
Canadian inventor Sandford Fleming suggests 24 world time zones.	World time zones are accepted.

Daylight saving time

In 1907 English builder William Willett suggested that Great Britain begin using **daylight saving time** (DST). Moving the clocks forward an hour during the summer would shift daylight hours from morning to evening. At first, most people laughed at the idea. But on April 30, 1916, Germany and Austria did just that. The next October, they returned to standard time. They moved forward again the next summer, and so on. Many other countries did the same.

▼ U.S. inventor and politician Benjamin Franklin first suggested daylight saving time in 1784.

1784
The U.S. inventor and politician Benjamin Franklin suggests daylight saving time.

22

1800

1907
English builder William Willett pushes for DST in England.

1900

This clockmaker needs to reset all the clocks in his shop when the time changes.

Britain adopted DST on May 21, 1916. In 1917 Australia and Newfoundland did, too. The United States waited until 1918. Today, about 70 countries use DST. However, countries near the **equator** do not change their clocks. Their days and nights are about the same all year long.

Disagreeing over DST

Many people enjoy the longer summer evenings. Some people believe DST saves energy. Ideally, people will use fewer lights and watch less television in the evening because they will be outside.

On the other hand, some people argue that DST does not add more hours to the day. It shifts daylight hours from morning to evening, so it does not really save energy. Several studies are underway to see whether or not DST saves energy.

Cow time ✔

Cows have a difficult time changing to DST. Some farmers help their cows adjust to DST by changing their milking schedule gradually.

1916
Germany, Austria, Great Britain, and other countries adopt DST.

1917
Australia and Newfoundland adopt DST.

1918
The United States adopts DST.

23

Time Travel

▲ These animals were painted on a cave wall in Africa in about 2000 BCE. That is over 4,000 years ago.

In some ways, we are all time travelers. We are born in one time, and with each new day we travel into the future. We can visit the past by going to museums or reading books, diaries, and letters from older periods. Old movies, paintings, and drawings also help us see into the past. But how do we go to the future?

Time capsules

Time capsules are a way of telling future people about life today. A time capsule is a container that includes items from the present. It might include voice or music recordings. It might include photos or everyday objects such as dishes, jewelry, pens, or pencils. If you were putting together a time capsule, what would you include?

Visiting the future

Science fiction writers help us to imagine the future. They use science to tell stories about other worlds or other times. Some science fiction writers imagine time machines. But there are no working time machines today.

Time travel is closely connected with space travel. Some scientists believe that by traveling through a black hole (a collapsed star), people will reach the future. Others suggest that a spacecraft could use certain forces in space to pull itself into the past. These are exciting ideas. But for now we will have to use our imaginations to visit other times.

▼ This time capsule is being buried as part of the 1939 World's Fair in New York City.

Atomic clocks

The first **atomic clock** was built in 1948. It used atoms, the tiny parts that make up all things, to tell the exact time. Atomic clocks keep better time than any other clocks. Scientists believe that atomic clocks will lose less than one second every million years. The first atomic clocks were expensive. Today, most people can afford to buy an atomic clock.

Atomic clocks will guide us into the future. Global Positioning Systems (systems that help cars and airplanes find their way) and the Internet depend on atomic clocks. So does space exploration.

▼ This 1959 photo shows U.S. scientist Harold Lyons looking at an atomic clock being built for the U.S. space program.

Time matters

Time has always been important to people. Calendars helped ancient farmers know when to plant crops. Today, clocks and watches help us plan our days. We carry time around with us on our wrists. Whether we are rich or poor, young or old, we all have the same 24 hours each day. How do you use your time? Do you spend it wisely or do you waste it? It is your time to use.

Time words ✔

According to the writers of *The Oxford English Dictionary*, the most commonly used noun in the English language is time. (A noun is a word that refers to a person, place, or thing.) The second most commonly used noun is person, followed by year, way, and day.

▼ The World Time Clock in Berlin, Germany, gives the time in each of the world's 24 **time zones**.

Timeline

(These dates are often approximations.)

13,700 BYA
The "dawn of time" occurs.

4,500 BYA-544 MYA
The Precambrian **Era** begins and ends.

10,000 BYA

3000 BCE
Builders begin creating Stonehenge.

3500 BCE
The Egyptians use **obelisks** to tell the time.

4241 BCE
The Egyptians use a **lunar calendar.**

3000 BCE   4000 BCE

2772 BCE
The Egyptians switch to a **solar calendar.**

753 BCE
The first Roman calendar is used, with a seven-day week.

2000 BCE   1000 BCE

1656
Dutch astronomer Christiaan Huygens invents the pendulum clock.

1582
The Gregorian calendar is created.

1509
German locksmith Peter Henlein uses springs to power clocks.

1600   1500

1752
The Gregorian calendar is adopted in the American colonies and Great Britain.

1700   1750

1907
English builder William Willett pushes for DST in England.

1884
World time zones are accepted.

1882
Canadian inventor Sandford Fleming suggests 24 world time zones.

1873
The Gregorian calendar is adopted in Japan.

1900

1916
Germany, Austria, Britain, and other countries adopt DST.

1917
Australia and Newfoundland adopt DST.

1918
The United States adopts DST.

1948
The first atomic clock is built and used.

1949
The Gregorian calendar is fully adopted in China.

1950

28   This symbol shows where there is a change of scale in the timeline, or where a long period of time with no noted events has been left out.

544-245 MYA
The Paleozoic Era begins and ends.

1000 MYA → → 500 MYA

1.8 MYA
Human beings appear.

65 MYA
The Cenozoic Era begins. It continues through today.

245-65 MYA
The Mesozoic Era begins and ends.

1 MYA

46 BCE
The Julian calendar is created.

200-1300 CE
The Chinese use water clocks.

0 → 1200 CE

1285
The first ticking clocks are built.

1400 ← 1300

1761
British inventor John Harrison invents a clock for use at sea.

1784
U.S. inventor and politician Benjamin Franklin suggests daylight saving time (DST).

→ 1800

1852
Britain begins using standard time.

← 1850 ←

1999
Scientists develop an improved atomic clock.

TODAY
Computers and cell phones often serve as clocks and watches.

→ → 2000

BYA means "billion years ago."
MYA means "million years ago."

29

Glossary

alternating current electricity
electricity that travels through wires from power stations into people's homes

astronomer scientist who studies the stars and planets. Astronomers study the cycles of the moon and Sun.

atomic clock clock that uses atoms, the tiny parts that make up all things. Atomic clocks keep more accurate time than any other clocks.

BCE meaning "before the common era." When this appears after a date, it refers to the time before the Christian religion began. BCE dates are always counted backwards.

biological clock internal cycle or rhythm that tells animals and people when to sleep, eat, wake, and other things. If your mom does not wake you up in the morning, your biological clock will.

CE meaning "common era." When this appears after a date, it refers to the time after the Christian religion began.

cell small unit that is a basic part of all living things. The human body is made up of billions of cells.

daylight saving time (DST) period when clocks are set ahead to provide more daylight in the evening. Daylight saving time begins in the spring.

equator imaginary line around Earth that is an equal distance from the North and South Poles. At the equator, there are 12 hours of light and 12 hours of darkness.

era period of time. Dinosaurs lived during the Mesozoic Era.

gear wheel with "teeth." In some clocks, gears move the clock hands forward.

geologic time period of time when Earth was forming and developing. Studying geologic time helps scientists understand Earth's past.

geologist scientist who studies Earth's surface. Geologists can work out the age of rocks.

lunar calendar calendar based on the cycles of the moon. The Egyptians used a lunar calendar.

mammal warm-blooded animal that feeds its young with milk and has a backbone and limbs. A dog is a mammal.

obelisk four-sided stone tower used to tell time. The ancient Egyptians built giant obelisks.

pendulum swinging arm. Grandfather clocks have a pendulum.

phase stage in a process. The phases of the moon repeat each month.

reptile cold-blooded animal that breathes air and usually has skin covered with scales or bony plates. Snakes, alligators, and lizards are reptiles.

solar calendar calendar based on the cycles of the sun. Solar calendars are more exact than lunar calendars.

time zone one of 24 divisions of Earth sharing the same time. Each time zone is one hour earlier or later than the one next to it.

Find Out More

Books

Formichelli, Linda, and W. Eric Martin. *Tools of Timekeeping: A Kid's Guide to the History and Science of Telling Time*. White River Junction, Vt.: Nomad, 2005.

Koscielniak, Bruce. *About Time: A First Look at Time and Clocks*. Boston: Houghton Mifflin, 2004.

Mandell, Muriel. *Simple Experiments in Time*. New York: Sterling, 2007.

Murrie, Steve, and Matthew Murrie. *Every Minute on Earth: Fun Facts That Happen Every 60 Seconds*. New York: Scholastic, 2007.

Websites

Learn more about geologic time.
www.ucmp.berkeley.edu/education/explorations/tours/geotime

Visit the website Clockworks: From Sundials to the Atomic Second.
www.britannica.com/clockworks/main.html

Play time-related games.
www.gamequarium.com/time.html

Visit the world clock.
www.timeanddate.com/worldclock

Index